Operation Allied Force: The Untold Story of NATO's Air Campaign Against Serbia

Copyright Page

TITLE: Operation Allied Force: The Untold Story of NATO's Air Campaign Against Serbia

1ST Edition

Table of Contents

Operation Allied Force: The Untold Story of NATO's Air Campaign Against Serbia

By Roberto Miguel Rodriguez

Chapter 1: Operation Allied Force: NATO's Air Campaign Against Serbia

The Origins and Justifications for Operation Allied Force

Operation Allied Force: The Untold Story of NATO's Air Campaign Against Serbia delves into the complexities and intricacies of one of the most significant military interventions in recent history. This subchapter titled "The Origins and Justifications for Operation Allied Force" aims to provide historians with a comprehensive understanding of the motivations and reasoning behind NATO's decision to launch the air campaign against Serbia.

The chapter begins by exploring the historical context that led to the outbreak of conflict in the Balkans. It highlights the tensions between Serbia and its neighboring countries and the escalating violence that threatened regional stability. The chapter then delves into the diplomatic challenges faced by NATO and its member countries as they sought to find a peaceful resolution to the crisis. It delves into the negotiations with Serbia and international allies, shedding light on the complexities of these discussions and the varying perspectives of the participating parties.

Moving on, the chapter sheds light on the role of technology in the air campaign. It provides an in-depth analysis of the advanced military technology utilized by NATO forces, including surveillance systems, precision-guided munitions, and air superiority capabilities. The impact of these technological advancements on the effectiveness of the campaign is thoroughly examined.

One of the key aspects explored in this chapter is the ethical and legal justifications for NATO's intervention in Serbia. The authors delve into the concept of the Responsibility to Protect (R2P) and how it was applied in this specific case. The chapter discusses the responsibility to prevent mass atrocities and the humanitarian intervention that took place. It raises questions about the ethical considerations and the legal framework under which NATO operated.

Additionally, the chapter investigates the role of media in shaping public perception of the air campaign. It explores the propaganda efforts employed by both NATO and Serbia, shedding light on the impact of media coverage on public opinion and the dissemination of information during the conflict.

Finally, the chapter assesses the long-term effects of Operation Allied Force on the Balkans region. It analyzes the political, economic, and social consequences of the air campaign, providing a comprehensive understanding of the lasting impact on regional stability.

In conclusion, this subchapter offers a detailed exploration of the origins and justifications for Operation Allied Force. It provides historians with a multi-faceted analysis of the decision-making process, the diplomatic challenges faced, the role of technology, the ethical and legal considerations, the media's influence, and the long-term impact on the Balkans region. Through this comprehensive examination, historians can gain a deeper understanding of this pivotal event in modern military history and its broader implications.

The Role of NATO in the Balkans

NATO's involvement in the Balkans during Operation Allied Force marked a significant turning point in the alliance's history. This subchapter aims to provide historians and those interested in Operation Allied Force with a comprehensive understanding of NATO's role in the Balkans. From diplomatic challenges to military strategies, this subchapter explores various aspects of NATO's intervention in Serbia.

One crucial aspect to consider is the targeting of military infrastructure. NATO's air campaign focused on specific targets and objectives, including strategic bridges, communication centers, and military installations. By disabling Serbia's military capabilities, NATO aimed to weaken the country's ability to wage war and force a diplomatic solution to the ongoing conflict.

However, the unintended consequences of the air campaign cannot be ignored. Civilian casualties and collateral damage were significant concerns. This subchapter delves into the impact on civilian populations and infrastructure, shedding light on the ethical and legal challenges faced by NATO during the campaign.

Diplomatic efforts and negotiations played a crucial role in achieving the mission's objectives. Analysis of the diplomatic challenges faced by NATO and its member countries during Operation Allied Force provides insight into the complex nature of international cooperation and the pursuit of political solutions in times of conflict.

Furthermore, the role of technology cannot be understated. This subchapter explores the advanced military technology deployed by NATO forces, including surveillance systems, precision-guided munitions, and air superiority capabilities. Understanding the role of technology in the air campaign is essential for comprehending the operational effectiveness and success of NATO's mission.

The concept of humanitarian intervention and the Responsibility to Protect (R2P) is another important aspect to consider. This subchapter engages with the ethical and legal justifications for NATO's intervention in Serbia, particularly focusing on the responsibility to prevent mass atrocities and the implications for future humanitarian interventions.

Media coverage and propaganda efforts also played a significant role in shaping public perception of the air campaign. Investigating the role of media and propaganda by both NATO and Serbia provides historians with an understanding of the information warfare that accompanied the military operations.

The long-term impact of Operation Allied Force on regional stability is assessed in this subchapter. Political, economic, and social consequences are analyzed to provide a comprehensive understanding of the campaign's effects on the Balkans region.

Additionally, this subchapter delves into NATO's military strategy and tactics. Analyzing the overarching military strategy employed by NATO during the air campaign, including the coordination of air assets, target selection, and operational effectiveness, helps historians assess the alliance's military capabilities.

Evaluating the lessons learned from Operation Allied Force and its impact on subsequent military doctrines and strategies is crucial in understanding the evolution of air warfare. This subchapter discusses the lessons learned and how they shaped future military operations.

Finally, exploring the involvement of non-NATO countries in the air campaign against Serbia is essential. This subchapter highlights the contributions of non-NATO countries, such as Australia and New Zealand, to the overall mission, emphasizing the importance of international cooperation in achieving the campaign's objectives.

In conclusion, this subchapter provides historians and those interested in Operation Allied Force with a comprehensive analysis of NATO's role in the Balkans. From military strategies to diplomatic challenges, this subchapter covers various aspects of the alliance's intervention in Serbia, offering invaluable insights into one of NATO's most significant operations in recent history.

The Objectives of the Air Campaign

In the subchapter titled "The Objectives of the Air Campaign," we delve into the specific targets and objectives of NATO's air campaign against Serbia during Operation Allied Force. This chapter aims to provide historians and readers interested in Operation Allied Force with a comprehensive understanding of the strategic goals and military tactics employed by NATO forces.

One of the primary objectives of the air campaign was to target military infrastructure in Serbia. NATO forces focused on strategic bridges, communication centers, and military installations to disrupt Serbia's ability to wage war and maintain control over Kosovo. By targeting these key assets, NATO aimed to weaken Serbia's military capabilities and compel them to negotiate a diplomatic solution.

However, as with any military campaign, unintended consequences occurred. Civilian casualties and collateral damage were inevitable. This chapter explores the impact of the air campaign on civilian populations and infrastructure, shedding light on the ethical and moral considerations of humanitarian intervention and the concept of Responsibility to Protect (R2P). It delves into the difficult balance between protecting civilians and achieving military objectives.

Diplomatic challenges and negotiations also played a crucial role in Operation Allied Force. NATO and its member countries engaged in diplomatic efforts with Serbia and international allies to find a peaceful resolution. The chapter analyzes these negotiations and the diplomatic strategies employed by NATO during the campaign.

The role of technology in the air campaign cannot be overlooked. Advanced military technology, including surveillance systems, precision-guided munitions, and air superiority capabilities, played a significant role in NATO's success. This chapter examines the technological advancements and their impact on the effectiveness of the air campaign.

Media coverage and propaganda are also investigated in this subchapter. The role of the media in shaping public perception of the air campaign, including propaganda efforts by both NATO and Serbia, are explored. This chapter aims to shed light on the influence of media coverage on public opinion and the portrayal of the conflict.

Furthermore, the long-term effects of Operation Allied Force on regional stability in the Balkans are assessed. Political, economic, and social consequences are analyzed to gain an understanding of the broader impact of the air campaign.

The chapter also delves into NATO's military strategy and tactics. It evaluates the overarching military strategy employed by NATO, including the coordination of air assets, target selection, and operational effectiveness. Lessons learned from Operation Allied Force and its impact on subsequent military doctrines and strategies are also evaluated.

Lastly, the involvement of non-NATO countries in the air campaign against Serbia is explored. The contributions made by countries like Australia and New Zealand to the overall mission are highlighted, providing a comprehensive view of the international coalition formed during Operation Allied Force.

Overall, this subchapter aims to provide historians and readers interested in Operation Allied Force with a detailed analysis of the objectives, strategies, and impacts of NATO's air campaign against Serbia.

Chapter 2: Targeting Military Infrastructure: Focusing on the Specific Targets and Objectives of NATO's Air Campaign Against Serbia

Strategic Bridges: Disrupting Serbian Transportation Networks

During Operation Allied Force, NATO's air campaign against Serbia, one of the key targets was the disruption of Serbian transportation networks, particularly strategic bridges. This subchapter delves into the strategic importance of targeting these bridges, the objectives behind their destruction, and the impact it had on the overall campaign.

NATO recognized the critical role that transportation networks played in Serbia's military capabilities and its ability to sustain its forces. By targeting strategic bridges, NATO aimed to sever key supply routes, hinder troop movements, and impede the resupply of Serbian military installations. These bridges served as vital connections between different parts of the country, and their destruction significantly disrupted Serbia's transportation infrastructure.

The objectives of targeting these bridges were twofold. First, it aimed to limit the mobility and logistical capabilities of the Serbian military, thereby degrading its ability to launch offensive operations. Second, it aimed to isolate Serbian forces by cutting off their supply lines, forcing them into a weakened state and reducing their overall effectiveness.

The destruction of these bridges had a significant impact on the air campaign. It disrupted the Serbian military's ability to efficiently move troops and equipment, hampering their ability to respond to NATO airstrikes and weakening their defensive capabilities. Additionally, it put pressure on the Serbian leadership, as they had to divert resources towards repairing or rebuilding these vital infrastructure elements.

However, the destruction of strategic bridges also had unintended consequences. The disruption of transportation networks had a profound impact on civilian populations, who relied on these bridges for daily commute, trade, and access to essential services. It resulted in civilian casualties and collateral damage, raising ethical and legal concerns about the proportionality of the air campaign.

This subchapter explores the strategic rationale behind targeting bridges, the operational effectiveness of these strikes, and the ethical implications of disrupting civilian transportation networks. It also analyzes the long-term effects of these actions, including their impact on regional stability and the subsequent reconstruction efforts in Serbia.

By examining the disruption of Serbian transportation networks, this subchapter sheds light on the complexities and challenges faced by NATO during Operation Allied Force. It provides historians and enthusiasts with a comprehensive understanding of the air campaign's strategic objectives, its impact on civilian populations, and the lessons learned from this historic military operation.

Communication Centers: Severing Serbian Military Communication

During Operation Allied Force, NATO's air campaign against Serbia, communication centers played a crucial role in the Serbian military's command and control infrastructure. Targeting these centers became a key objective for the Alliance, as severing Serbian military communication would significantly hamper their ability to coordinate and carry out military operations.

NATO's strategy involved targeting communication centers through precision airstrikes, aiming to disrupt the Serbian military's ability to transmit vital information, receive orders, and coordinate their forces.

By severing their communication lines, NATO sought to degrade the Serbian military's situational awareness and their ability to effectively respond to the Alliance's air campaign.

The communication centers targeted by NATO were carefully selected based on their strategic importance and the potential impact their destruction would have on Serbian military operations. These centers served as the nerve centers of the Serbian military's command structure, relaying orders, intelligence, and coordinating the movements of troops and equipment.

Precision-guided munitions, such as laser-guided bombs and cruise missiles, were employed to strike these communication centers with minimal collateral damage. Advanced surveillance systems allowed NATO forces to gather intelligence on the locations of these centers, ensuring accurate target selection and minimizing the risk of civilian casualties.

The severing of Serbian military communication had a profound impact on the effectiveness of the Serbian military during the air campaign. Without the ability to transmit timely information and coordinate their forces, the Serbian military faced significant challenges in responding to NATO's airstrikes and coordinating their own operations.

The targeting of communication centers also demonstrated NATO's advanced military technology and its ability to disrupt enemy command and control systems. This showcased the evolving nature of air warfare and the increasing importance of information dominance in modern conflicts.

The success of NATO's efforts to sever Serbian military communication highlights the importance of targeting military infrastructure in achieving strategic objectives. By disrupting the enemy's ability to communicate and coordinate, NATO was able to gain a significant advantage in the air campaign.

In conclusion, the targeting of communication centers during Operation Allied Force played a vital role in severing Serbian military communication and degrading their ability to effectively respond to NATO's air campaign. This subchapter sheds light on the strategic importance of communication centers, the precision airstrikes employed by NATO, and the impact of severing Serbian military communication on the overall success of the air campaign. Historians studying Operation Allied Force and the evolution of air warfare will find this subchapter invaluable in understanding the significance of targeting communication centers in modern conflict.

Military Installations: Weakening Serbian Defense Capabilities

During Operation Allied Force, NATO's air campaign against Serbia, one of the primary objectives was to weaken the Serbian defense capabilities by targeting their military installations. This subchapter delves into the specific targets and objectives of NATO's air campaign, shedding light on the strategic bridges, communication centers, and military installations that were meticulously selected for attack.

NATO's air campaign aimed to disrupt Serbia's ability to launch offensive operations and maintain control over Kosovo. By targeting military installations, NATO sought to degrade the Serbian defense capabilities and cripple their command and control systems. This subchapter provides a comprehensive analysis of the targets chosen by NATO, highlighting the rationale behind their selection and the impact of these strikes on the Serbian military.

The destruction of strategic bridges played a crucial role in hampering the mobility and logistical capabilities of the Serbian military. By severing key transportation routes, NATO hindered the movement of troops and supplies, effectively impeding the Serbian defense efforts. Communication centers, on the other hand, were targeted to disrupt the command hierarchy and disrupt the flow of information within the Serbian military apparatus.

Moreover, this subchapter explores the consequences of NATO's air campaign on civilian populations and infrastructure. While the primary focus was on military installations, unintended civilian casualties and collateral damage occurred. The chapter delves into the ethical and legal implications of these unintended consequences, shedding light on the delicate balance between achieving military objectives and minimizing harm to non-combatants.

Furthermore, this subchapter delves into the diplomatic challenges and negotiations undertaken by NATO and its member countries during Operation Allied Force. It analyzes the diplomatic efforts made to garner international support, negotiate with Serbia, and maintain cohesion among the coalition forces. The subchapter also evaluates the effectiveness of these diplomatic endeavors in achieving NATO's objectives.

In conclusion, this subchapter provides historians and enthusiasts of Operation Allied Force with a comprehensive understanding of NATO's air campaign against Serbia and its specific objectives of targeting military installations. By exploring the rationale behind target selection and analyzing the consequences of these strikes, this subchapter sheds light on the strategic thinking and decision-making processes that shaped this pivotal military operation.

Chapter 3: Civilian Casualties and Collateral Damage: Exploring the Unintended Consequences of the Air Campaign

The Impact on Civilian Populations

During Operation Allied Force, NATO's air campaign against Serbia, the impact on civilian populations cannot be overlooked. While the primary objective of the campaign was to weaken and degrade Serbia's military capabilities, there were unintended consequences that affected civilians and their infrastructure.

One of the key issues that arose during the campaign was civilian casualties and collateral damage. Despite efforts to minimize civilian harm, the precision-guided munitions used by NATO forces were not always foolproof. There were instances where civilian areas were mistakenly targeted or where the destruction of military infrastructure led to unintended damage to nearby civilian buildings and infrastructure.

The impact on civilian populations was not limited to physical harm alone. The air campaign disrupted the lives of ordinary civilians, causing fear and uncertainty. Communication centers, essential for everyday life, were targeted, leading to disruptions in communication networks and services. This made it difficult for civilians to access vital information, contact loved ones, or receive emergency assistance.

The air campaign also had diplomatic challenges and negotiations. NATO and its member countries had to navigate the complexities of international diplomacy while conducting military operations. Negotiations with Serbia and international allies were crucial in managing the fallout from the air campaign and ensuring a peaceful resolution.

Technology played a significant role in the air campaign, with NATO forces employing advanced military technology. Surveillance systems helped identify and track targets, while precision-guided munitions allowed for accurate strikes on military infrastructure. The use of air superiority capabilities also ensured NATO's dominance in the skies.

However, the use of such technology also raised ethical and legal questions. The concept of Responsibility to Protect (R2P) came into play, as NATO justified its intervention in Serbia to prevent mass atrocities. This intervention, though humanitarian in nature, raised concerns about the boundaries of sovereignty and the use of force for humanitarian purposes.

Media coverage and propaganda played a significant role in shaping public perception of the air campaign. Both NATO and Serbia engaged in propaganda efforts to influence public opinion. The media's portrayal of the campaign, whether accurate or biased, had far-reaching consequences in terms of public support and international perception.

The impact of Operation Allied Force extended beyond Serbia itself. The air campaign had significant implications for regional stability in the Balkans. The political, economic, and social consequences of the campaign were far-reaching, shaping the future of the region.

The military strategy and tactics employed by NATO during the air campaign were critical to its success. The coordination of air assets, target selection, and operational effectiveness played a crucial role in achieving NATO's objectives.

Operation Allied Force provided valuable lessons for future military doctrines and strategies. The campaign's impact on subsequent military operations and the evolution of air warfare cannot be understated. The lessons learned from this operation continue to shape military thinking and decision-making.

Lastly, the involvement of non-NATO countries, such as Australia and New Zealand, in the air campaign against Serbia was significant. Their contributions to the overall mission demonstrated the broad international support for NATO's efforts and the importance of collective security in addressing regional conflicts.

In conclusion, the impact on civilian populations during Operation Allied Force was a multifaceted issue. The unintended consequences of the air campaign, including civilian casualties and collateral damage, disrupted infrastructure, and diplomatic challenges, highlight the complexities of military interventions. It is crucial for historians to examine these aspects to gain a comprehensive understanding of NATO's air campaign against Serbia and its broader implications for international relations and military strategies.

Destruction of Infrastructure and Essential Services

During Operation Allied Force, NATO's air campaign against Serbia, one of the primary objectives was the destruction of key infrastructure and essential services that supported Serbia's military capabilities. This subchapter delves into the specific targets and objectives of NATO's air campaign, shedding light on the strategic bridges, communication centers, and military installations that were targeted.

The destruction of strategic bridges played a crucial role in disrupting Serbia's military operations. By rendering these vital transportation arteries impassable, NATO aimed to impede the movement of Serbian troops and supplies, ultimately hampering their ability to wage war. Additionally, communication centers were targeted to disrupt Serbia's command and control capabilities, further weakening their ability to coordinate military operations effectively.

However, the destruction of infrastructure and essential services had unintended consequences, resulting in civilian casualties and collateral damage. As NATO forces targeted military installations located in close proximity to civilian areas, the air campaign unintentionally caused harm to non-combatants and vital civilian infrastructure. This subchapter explores the moral and ethical dilemmas posed by these unintended consequences, as well as the measures taken by NATO to mitigate civilian harm.

Furthermore, this subchapter analyzes the diplomatic challenges and negotiations that took place during Operation Allied Force. It delves into the efforts made by NATO and its member countries to engage in diplomatic dialogue with Serbia and international allies, seeking to find a peaceful resolution to the conflict. The subchapter also examines the impact of these diplomatic efforts on the course of the air campaign and the subsequent outcomes.

The role of technology in the air campaign is another significant aspect explored in this subchapter. It examines the advanced military technology employed by NATO forces, such as surveillance systems, precision-guided munitions, and air superiority capabilities. This analysis sheds light on how technological advancements influenced the effectiveness and precision of the air campaign.

Lastly, this subchapter discusses the long-term consequences of Operation Allied Force on regional stability in the Balkans. It assesses the political, economic, and social impact of the air campaign, exploring how it shaped the region's trajectory in the aftermath of the conflict.

In conclusion, this subchapter provides a comprehensive analysis of the destruction of infrastructure and essential services during Operation Allied Force. It examines the specific targets and objectives of NATO's air campaign, the unintended consequences on civilian populations and infrastructure, diplomatic challenges and negotiations, the role of technology, and the long-term impact on regional stability. Historians and those interested in Operation Allied Force will gain valuable insights into the complexities of this significant military campaign and its far-reaching implications.

Humanitarian Concerns and Aid Efforts

During Operation Allied Force, NATO's air campaign against Serbia, humanitarian concerns and aid efforts played a crucial role in mitigating the impact on civilian populations and infrastructure. While the primary objective of the campaign was to target military infrastructure and cripple Serbia's ability to wage war, unintended consequences such as civilian casualties and collateral damage necessitated humanitarian intervention.

NATO and its member countries recognized the ethical and legal justifications for their intervention in Serbia, particularly in light of the Responsibility to Protect (R2P) doctrine. R2P asserts that states have a responsibility to prevent mass atrocities, and the air campaign was seen as a necessary step to protect the civilian population from the brutalities of the Serbian regime.

A significant challenge faced by NATO was minimizing civilian casualties and collateral damage. Despite the use of precision-guided munitions and advanced surveillance systems, there were instances where civilian targets were mistakenly hit. NATO made efforts to minimize harm by employing strict target selection processes, ensuring that only military infrastructure vital to Serbia's war effort was targeted.

In addition to targeting military installations, NATO also focused on aid efforts to alleviate the suffering of the civilian population. Humanitarian aid was provided to displaced persons and refugees, ensuring they had access to food, shelter, and medical assistance. NATO member countries, as well as non-NATO countries such as Australia and New Zealand, played a crucial role in providing humanitarian assistance and support.

Media coverage and propaganda played a significant role in shaping public perception of the air campaign. Both NATO and Serbia engaged in propaganda efforts to gain support and legitimacy for their actions. NATO sought to portray its intervention as a necessary humanitarian intervention, while Serbia used propaganda to garner sympathy and portray itself as a victim of aggression.

The long-term impact of Operation Allied Force on the Balkans region was significant. The air campaign led to political, economic, and social consequences that shaped the region's future. The intervention ultimately contributed to the downfall of the Serbian regime and paved the way for political stability and the establishment of democratic institutions.

Operation Allied Force also had a profound impact on the evolution of air warfare. Lessons learned from the campaign influenced subsequent military doctrines and strategies. The use of advanced military technology, such as precision-guided munitions and air superiority capabilities, showcased the effectiveness of air power in modern warfare.

In conclusion, humanitarian concerns and aid efforts were integral aspects of Operation Allied Force. NATO's intervention in Serbia was driven by a sense of responsibility to protect civilians from mass atrocities. While the campaign had unintended consequences, efforts were made to minimize harm and provide humanitarian assistance to those affected. The long-term impact of the campaign shaped the Balkans region and influenced the evolution of air warfare.

Chapter 4: Diplomatic Challenges and Negotiations: Analyzing the Efforts Made by NATO and its Member Countries

Negotiations with Serbia

During Operation Allied Force, NATO faced numerous diplomatic challenges as it sought to achieve its objectives and bring an end to the conflict in Serbia. Negotiations with Serbia and international allies played a crucial role in shaping the outcome of the air campaign. This subchapter will delve into the intricacies of these negotiations and shed light on their significance in the larger context of the operation.

From the outset, NATO made diplomatic efforts to find a peaceful resolution to the conflict. However, negotiations with Serbia proved to be difficult due to the entrenched positions held by both sides. Serbia, under President Slobodan Milosevic, was reluctant to yield to NATO's demands, leading to prolonged discussions and a stalemate in the early stages of the operation.

Diplomatic pressure was exerted on Serbia through various channels, including economic sanctions and political isolation. NATO member countries worked in tandem to present a united front and emphasize the importance of a peaceful resolution. The United Nations played a crucial role in facilitating negotiations, with key diplomatic figures engaging in shuttle diplomacy between NATO headquarters and Belgrade.

As the air campaign intensified, negotiations took on a renewed sense of urgency. NATO sought to leverage its military advantage to convince Serbia to come to the negotiating table. The destruction of strategic bridges, communication centers, and military installations had a twofold purpose: to degrade Serbia's military capabilities and to demonstrate NATO's resolve.

Finally, after weeks of intense negotiations, a breakthrough was achieved. A diplomatic agreement, known as the Kumanovo Agreement, was reached on June 9, 1999. Under this agreement, Serbia agreed to withdraw its forces from Kosovo, paving the way for the deployment of an international peacekeeping force.

The negotiations with Serbia during Operation Allied Force underscored the delicate balance between military force and diplomacy. While the air campaign was instrumental in bringing Serbia to the negotiating table, it was ultimately the diplomatic efforts that led to a resolution. The lessons learned from these negotiations have had a lasting impact on subsequent military doctrines and strategies, emphasizing the importance of a comprehensive approach that combines military force with diplomatic initiatives.

In conclusion, the negotiations with Serbia during Operation Allied Force were a critical aspect of the air campaign. They demonstrated the complexities and challenges of diplomatic efforts in a conflict zone, while also highlighting the importance of finding a balance between military force and diplomacy. By exploring these negotiations, historians can gain valuable insights into the broader dynamics of the conflict and the role of diplomacy in achieving peace.

International Allies and Diplomatic Support

Throughout Operation Allied Force, NATO relied on the support and cooperation of its international allies to achieve its objectives in the air campaign against Serbia. This subchapter explores the crucial role played by these allies and the diplomatic efforts undertaken during the operation.

NATO's air campaign against Serbia was a multinational endeavor, with countries from around the world contributing their military assets and diplomatic support. Historians examining this period will delve into the intricate web of alliances and negotiations that facilitated the operation's success.

One key aspect to explore is the diplomatic challenges faced by NATO and its member countries. The book will analyze the negotiations with Serbia, shedding light on the complexities of reaching a diplomatic resolution while conducting a military campaign. It will also examine the role of international allies in these negotiations and their efforts to bring about a peaceful resolution.

Furthermore, historians will assess the impact of diplomatic support on the overall outcome of the campaign. The book will delve into how diplomatic efforts influenced the targeting of military infrastructure, including strategic bridges, communication centers, and military installations. It will also explore how diplomatic negotiations affected the decision-making process and the overall effectiveness of NATO's military strategy.

In addition, the book will highlight the contributions of non-NATO countries, such as Australia and New Zealand, and their involvement in the air campaign. It will explore their specific roles and contributions to the overall mission, showcasing the global nature of Operation Allied Force and the international cooperation that underpinned its success.

Overall, this subchapter will provide historians with a comprehensive understanding of the international allies and diplomatic support that shaped Operation Allied Force. By examining the negotiations, diplomatic challenges, and contributions of non-NATO countries, it will shed light on the intricate web of alliances and the crucial role of diplomacy in achieving military objectives. This analysis will contribute to a deeper understanding of the complexities and nuances of this historic air campaign, its diplomatic dimensions, and its lasting impact on international relations.

Challenges and Obstacles in Achieving Diplomatic Objectives

Throughout Operation Allied Force, NATO faced numerous challenges and obstacles in achieving its diplomatic objectives. This subchapter delves into the complexities and difficulties encountered during the diplomatic efforts made by NATO and its member countries.

The chapter begins by examining the initial negotiations with Serbia and international allies. Diplomatic channels were utilized in an attempt to peacefully resolve the conflict, but these efforts were met with resistance and reluctance from Serbian leaders. The chapter highlights the strained diplomatic relations and the challenges faced by NATO in navigating these complex negotiations.

Furthermore, the subchapter explores the role of diplomacy in mitigating civilian casualties and collateral damage. The unintended consequences of the air campaign, including the impact on civilian populations and infrastructure, posed significant diplomatic challenges for NATO. The subchapter delves into the ethical and legal justifications for NATO's intervention in Serbia, focusing on the concept of Responsibility to Protect (R2P) and the responsibility to prevent mass atrocities. It analyzes the delicate balance between achieving military objectives and minimizing civilian harm, and the diplomatic challenges that arose from this balancing act.

Another key aspect discussed in this subchapter is the impact of media coverage and propaganda on shaping public perception of the air campaign. NATO and Serbia both engaged in extensive propaganda efforts, utilizing the media to advance their respective narratives. The subchapter investigates the role of media in the conflict and the challenges faced by NATO in countering Serbian propaganda.

Additionally, the subchapter assesses the long-term effects of Operation Allied Force on regional stability in the Balkans. The political, economic, and social consequences of the military intervention are analyzed, shedding light on the challenges faced by NATO in restoring stability and rebuilding the region.

Lastly, the subchapter evaluates the lessons learned from Operation Allied Force and its impact on subsequent military doctrines and strategies. The subchapter explores the evolving nature of air warfare and the technological advancements that shaped NATO's military strategy. It also examines the involvement of non-NATO countries, such as Australia and New Zealand, and their contributions to the overall mission.

By delving into the challenges and obstacles faced by NATO in achieving its diplomatic objectives, this subchapter provides historians with a comprehensive understanding of the complexities of Operation Allied Force and its long-lasting impact on the Balkans and international diplomacy.

Chapter 5: Role of Technology in the Air Campaign: Examining the Advanced Military Technology Used by NATO Forces

Surveillance Systems: Gathering Intelligence and Targeting Capabilities

Throughout Operation Allied Force, NATO forces relied heavily on surveillance systems to gather intelligence and enhance their targeting capabilities. These systems played a crucial role in identifying strategic bridges, communication centers, and military installations that were key to the success of the air campaign against Serbia.

One of the most significant surveillance systems used by NATO forces was aerial reconnaissance. Sophisticated aircraft equipped with state-of-the-art sensors and cameras were deployed to collect real-time imagery and intelligence. These aerial platforms provided invaluable information about Serbian military activities, enabling NATO to identify and target critical infrastructure with precision.

In addition to aerial reconnaissance, NATO also utilized unmanned aerial vehicles (UAVs) to gather intelligence. These unmanned aircraft, commonly known as drones, allowed NATO forces to monitor Serbian military movements and activities in real-time without putting pilots at risk. The use of UAVs greatly enhanced NATO's surveillance capabilities and provided a constant stream of valuable information to inform targeting decisions.

Furthermore, NATO relied on ground-based surveillance systems to augment its intelligence-gathering efforts. These systems, such as radar installations and satellite imagery, provided a comprehensive view of the battlefield and allowed NATO forces to monitor Serbian military activities on a 24/7 basis. The integration of these ground-based surveillance systems with the aerial platforms and UAVs ensured a comprehensive and accurate picture of the situation on the ground.

The intelligence gathered through these surveillance systems played a crucial role in targeting military infrastructure during the air campaign. By identifying and prioritizing key targets, NATO forces were able to disrupt Serbian military capabilities and degrade their ability to wage war effectively. This targeted approach minimized the risk of civilian casualties and collateral damage, although unintended consequences did occur.

The use of advanced surveillance systems and the intelligence they provided also demonstrated the evolving nature of air warfare. Operation Allied Force showcased the increasing reliance on technology and precision-guided munitions to minimize collateral damage and achieve strategic objectives. The success of the air campaign against Serbia highlighted the effectiveness of these systems in gathering intelligence and targeting military infrastructure.

In conclusion, the surveillance systems used by NATO forces during Operation Allied Force played a pivotal role in gathering intelligence and enhancing targeting capabilities. Aerial reconnaissance, unmanned aerial vehicles, and ground-based surveillance systems provided real-time information that informed the strategic decisions of NATO forces. The use of advanced technology and precision-guided munitions showcased the evolving nature of air warfare and its reliance on surveillance systems to achieve objectives with minimal collateral damage.

Precision-Guided Munitions: Ensuring Accurate Strikes

Operation Allied Force: The Untold Story of NATO's Air Campaign Against Serbia

Precision-guided munitions played a crucial role in ensuring accurate strikes during NATO's air campaign against Serbia. These advanced weapons systems enabled NATO forces to minimize collateral damage and civilian casualties, while effectively targeting military infrastructure and achieving strategic objectives.

By utilizing precision-guided munitions, such as guided bombs and missiles, NATO forces were able to hit specific targets with remarkable accuracy. Unlike traditional weapons, which relied on area saturation and the inherent imprecision of unguided munitions, precision-guided munitions allowed for precise and surgical strikes. This greatly reduced the risk of unintended harm to civilian populations and infrastructure, while maximizing the destruction of military installations and strategic bridges.

The use of precision-guided munitions also showcased the role of technology in modern warfare. Surveillance systems, such as drones and satellites, provided real-time intelligence to NATO forces, enabling them to identify and track targets with unprecedented accuracy. This information was then used to guide the munitions, ensuring that they would hit their intended targets with precision.

Furthermore, precision-guided munitions enhanced NATO's air superiority capabilities. By neutralizing enemy air defenses and infrastructure, such as communication centers, NATO forces were able to establish air dominance, allowing for unimpeded operations and the protection of friendly forces.

However, the use of precision-guided munitions did not come without challenges. The evolving nature of warfare necessitated constant adaptation and improvement in technology and tactics. Lessons learned from Operation Allied Force led to the development of more advanced and capable precision-guided munitions, further enhancing the effectiveness of future military campaigns.

Moreover, the ethical and legal implications of using precision-guided munitions were also subject to scrutiny. The responsibility to protect (R2P) concept, which justified NATO's intervention in Serbia, required careful consideration of the potential impact on civilian populations and infrastructure. While precision-guided munitions minimized collateral damage, the unintended consequences of the air campaign still raised concerns about civilian casualties and the overall humanitarian impact.

In conclusion, precision-guided munitions played a crucial role in ensuring accurate strikes during NATO's air campaign against Serbia. These advanced weapons systems enabled NATO forces to effectively target military infrastructure while minimizing collateral damage and civilian casualties. The use of precision-guided munitions showcased the role of technology in modern warfare and led to the development of more advanced munitions in subsequent military doctrines and strategies. However, the ethical and legal implications of their use remained a subject of debate, highlighting the need for careful consideration of the responsibility to protect civilian populations.

Air Superiority Capabilities: Maintaining Dominance in the Skies

In the subchapter titled "Air Superiority Capabilities: Maintaining Dominance in the Skies," we delve into the critical role played by air superiority capabilities in NATO's air campaign against Serbia during Operation Allied Force. This section explores the advanced military technology utilized by NATO forces, including surveillance systems, precision-guided munitions, and the strategic importance of air superiority.

NATO's air campaign against Serbia was a demonstration of the alliance's commitment to maintaining dominance in the skies. The air superiority capabilities employed by NATO forces played a pivotal role in achieving their objectives. These capabilities allowed NATO to gain control of the airspace, neutralize Serbian air defenses, and establish a safe operating environment for conducting precision strikes on strategic targets.

One of the key technological advancements utilized by NATO forces was the deployment of advanced surveillance systems. These systems, such as unmanned aerial vehicles (UAVs) and reconnaissance aircraft, provided real-time intelligence and situational awareness to NATO commanders. This enabled them to accurately identify and target Serbian military infrastructure, including strategic bridges, communication centers, and military installations.

Precision-guided munitions were another crucial component of NATO's air superiority capabilities. These highly accurate weapons minimized collateral damage and civilian casualties by precisely targeting specific military objectives. Guided by advanced targeting systems, such as laser-guided bombs and GPS-guided missiles, NATO forces were able to effectively neutralize Serbian military assets while minimizing unintended consequences.

Achieving and maintaining air superiority was not without challenges. Serbian air defenses posed a significant threat to NATO aircraft, and NATO's air superiority capabilities were deployed to counter this threat. Advanced fighter aircraft, such as the F-15 and F-16, equipped with state-of-the-art radar and electronic warfare systems, were utilized to neutralize Serbian anti-aircraft systems. The coordination and integration of these capabilities ensured the protection of NATO aircraft and their ability to conduct successful operations.

The subchapter also explores the long-term impact of Operation Allied Force on the evolution of air warfare. The lessons learned from this campaign influenced subsequent military doctrines and strategies, highlighting the importance of air superiority capabilities in future conflicts. The advancements made in surveillance systems, precision-guided munitions, and air defense technologies continue to shape the way modern air campaigns are conducted.

In conclusion, the subchapter "Air Superiority Capabilities: Maintaining Dominance in the Skies" provides historians and enthusiasts of Operation Allied Force with an in-depth analysis of the advanced military technology and tactics employed by NATO forces during the air campaign against Serbia. It highlights the crucial role played by air superiority capabilities in achieving NATO's objectives and shaping the future of air warfare.

Chapter 6: Humanitarian Intervention and the Responsibility to Protect (R2P)

The Ethical and Legal Justifications for NATO's Intervention

In the subchapter "The Ethical and Legal Justifications for NATO's Intervention," we delve into the complex moral and legal framework that underpinned NATO's decision to intervene in the conflict between Serbia and Kosovo. This chapter aims to provide historians and enthusiasts of Operation Allied Force with a comprehensive understanding of the ethical and legal justifications behind NATO's intervention.

The chapter begins by exploring the concept of humanitarian intervention and the Responsibility to Protect (R2P) doctrine. We delve into the ethical arguments that NATO member states put forth to justify their intervention, focusing on the responsibility to prevent mass atrocities and protect civilian populations. By examining the legal justifications, including the invocation of Article 5 of the North Atlantic Treaty, we shed light on the legal basis for NATO's intervention.

We then analyze the specific targets and objectives of NATO's air campaign against Serbia. From strategic bridges and communication centers to military installations, we investigate the military infrastructure that NATO forces targeted. By examining the military rationale behind these targets, we provide historians with a comprehensive understanding of NATO's strategic objectives.

Another crucial aspect we explore is the unintended consequences of the air campaign, including civilian casualties and collateral damage. We critically analyze the impact of NATO's actions on civilian populations and infrastructure, shedding light on the ethical implications of the campaign.

Furthermore, this chapter delves into the diplomatic challenges and negotiations faced by NATO during Operation Allied Force. We analyze the diplomatic efforts made by NATO and its member countries to resolve the conflict through negotiations with Serbia and international allies. By examining the diplomatic intricacies, we shed light on the challenges faced by NATO in maintaining a united front.

Additionally, we explore the role of advanced military technology in the air campaign, including surveillance systems, precision-guided munitions, and air superiority capabilities. By examining the technological advancements employed by NATO forces, we provide a comprehensive analysis of how technology shaped the outcome of the conflict.

Lastly, we discuss the impact of media coverage and propaganda on public perception of the air campaign. Investigating the role of media in shaping public opinion, we explore the propaganda efforts employed by both NATO and Serbia, shedding light on the information war that accompanied the conflict.

This subchapter aims to provide historians with a comprehensive understanding of the ethical and legal justifications for NATO's intervention in Operation Allied Force. By exploring these aspects, we contribute to the broader understanding of the conflict and its long-term implications on regional stability, military strategy, and the evolution of air warfare.

The Responsibility to Prevent Mass Atrocities

During Operation Allied Force, NATO's air campaign against Serbia, one of the key ethical and legal justifications for intervention was the concept of the Responsibility to Protect (R2P). This subchapter explores the responsibility of the international community to prevent mass atrocities and the role it played in NATO's decision to intervene in Serbia.

The R2P principle asserts that states have a responsibility to protect their populations from mass atrocities such as genocide, war crimes, ethnic cleansing, and crimes against humanity. However, when a state fails to fulfill this responsibility, the international community has a duty to intervene to protect the affected populations. This principle was crucial in justifying NATO's intervention in Serbia, as the Serbian government under Slobodan Milosevic was responsible for widespread human rights abuses and crimes against ethnic Albanians in Kosovo.

The subchapter delves into the historical context of the conflict, highlighting the escalating tensions between the Serbian government and the ethnic Albanian population in Kosovo. It examines the failure of diplomatic efforts to resolve the crisis, leading to a situation where military intervention became the only viable option to prevent further mass atrocities.

Furthermore, the subchapter explores the challenges faced by NATO in implementing the R2P principle. It discusses the legal justifications for intervention, including the authorization from the United Nations Security Council and the invocation of humanitarian intervention. It also analyzes the ethical considerations surrounding the use of force and the potential for civilian casualties and collateral damage.

The subchapter also highlights the importance of media coverage in shaping public perception of the air campaign and the propaganda efforts employed by both NATO and Serbia. It investigates how the media influenced international opinion and affected the support for NATO's intervention.

Finally, the subchapter concludes by examining the long-term impact of Operation Allied Force on the Balkans region. It assesses the political, economic, and social consequences of the intervention, including the establishment of the United Nations Interim Administration Mission in Kosovo (UNMIK) and the subsequent declaration of Kosovo's independence.

Overall, this subchapter provides historians with a comprehensive analysis of the responsibility to prevent mass atrocities during Operation Allied Force. It explores the ethical and legal justifications for NATO's intervention, the challenges faced in implementing the R2P principle, and the long-term consequences of the air campaign on the Balkans region. By examining these aspects, historians can gain a deeper understanding of the complexities of humanitarian intervention and its implications for future conflicts.

Balancing Humanitarian Concerns with National Sovereignty

In the complex landscape of international conflicts, striking a balance between humanitarian concerns and national sovereignty has always been a delicate task. Nowhere was this challenge more evident than during Operation Allied Force, NATO's air campaign against Serbia. As historians delve into the untold story of this campaign, it is essential to examine how NATO grappled with the ethical and legal considerations surrounding humanitarian intervention while respecting the principles of national sovereignty.

At the heart of this subchapter lies the fundamental question: when does the international community have a responsibility to intervene in the affairs of a sovereign state? NATO's intervention in Serbia was grounded in the concept of the Responsibility to Protect (R2P), a principle that emphasizes the duty of nations to prevent mass atrocities. This subchapter explores the ethical and legal justifications for NATO's intervention, shedding light on the complex decision-making process that balanced the need for humanitarian action with the respect for national sovereignty.

Examining the unintended consequences of the air campaign also provides valuable insights. Civilian casualties and collateral damage were inevitable in any military operation of such magnitude, and NATO faced criticism for the impact on civilian populations and infrastructure. By exploring these unintended consequences, historians can analyze the ethical dilemmas faced by decision-makers and the efforts made to mitigate harm to civilians.

Diplomatic challenges and negotiations played a crucial role throughout Operation Allied Force. NATO and its member countries engaged in extensive diplomatic efforts to resolve the conflict peacefully, negotiating with Serbia and international allies. Understanding the intricacies of these diplomatic endeavors provides historians with a comprehensive view of the complexities inherent in balancing humanitarian concerns with national sovereignty.

Furthermore, the role of technology in the air campaign cannot be overlooked. The use of advanced military technology, such as precision-guided munitions and surveillance systems, significantly influenced the outcome of the conflict. Examining the role of technology allows historians to evaluate the impact of advancements in warfare on the balance between humanitarian concerns and national sovereignty.

As historians delve into the untold story of Operation Allied Force, it is crucial to explore the multifaceted aspects that revolve around balancing humanitarian concerns with national sovereignty. By analyzing the ethical, legal, diplomatic, and technological dimensions, a comprehensive understanding of the challenges faced by NATO and its member countries during this historic campaign can be achieved. Ultimately, this subchapter aims to shed light on valuable lessons learned and their influence on subsequent military doctrines, strategies, and the international community's approach to humanitarian interventions.

Chapter 7: Media Coverage and Propaganda: Investigating the Role of Media in Shaping Public Perception

Propaganda Efforts by NATO

During Operation Allied Force, NATO employed various propaganda efforts to shape public perception of the air campaign against Serbia. These efforts aimed to garner support for the intervention and justify NATO's actions to both domestic and international audiences. This subchapter delves into the role of media and propaganda in influencing public opinion and shaping the narrative surrounding the conflict.

NATO recognized the importance of controlling the media narrative and ensuring that its actions were portrayed in a positive light. The alliance utilized various communication channels, including press releases, interviews, and televised briefings, to disseminate information to the public. NATO officials strategically crafted messages to emphasize the humanitarian nature of the intervention, highlighting the need to protect civilian populations and prevent mass atrocities.

Additionally, NATO sought to discredit Serbia and its leadership through propaganda efforts. The alliance highlighted instances of Serbian aggression and human rights abuses, painting a negative image of the Serbian government and justifying the intervention as a necessary response to these actions. NATO also utilized intelligence reports and satellite imagery to support its claims and provide evidence of Serbian military activities.

However, Serbia also engaged in its own propaganda efforts, aiming to counter NATO's narrative and garner sympathy for its cause. Serbian media outlets portrayed NATO's intervention as an act of aggression and emphasized civilian casualties and collateral damage caused by the airstrikes. Serbia sought to evoke international outrage and rally support against NATO's actions.

The media played a crucial role in shaping public perception of the conflict. Both NATO and Serbia utilized media outlets to disseminate their respective messages and garner support for their positions. The audience was bombarded with conflicting narratives, making it challenging to discern the truth amidst the propaganda efforts of both sides.

Ultimately, the propaganda efforts by NATO and Serbia had a significant impact on public opinion and international support for the air campaign. Understanding the role of propaganda in shaping the narrative of Operation Allied Force is essential for historians seeking to analyze the motivations, justifications, and consequences of NATO's intervention in Serbia. By examining the propaganda efforts employed by NATO, historians can gain insight into the complexities of modern warfare and the challenges faced by military alliances in shaping public perception.

Propaganda Efforts by Serbia

Throughout the course of Operation Allied Force, Serbia employed various propaganda efforts to shape public perception and gain support for its cause. These efforts aimed to manipulate the media, disseminate false information, and evoke sympathy for Serbia's position. Understanding the role of propaganda in this conflict is essential for historians studying Operation Allied Force.

Serbia made extensive use of state-controlled media outlets to spread its narrative and demonize NATO forces. The government-controlled media disseminated false information, exaggerating civilian casualties and collateral damage caused by NATO airstrikes. This propaganda aimed to generate public outrage and undermine the legitimacy of NATO's intervention.

Furthermore, Serbia employed psychological warfare tactics to manipulate public sentiment. The government organized rallies and public demonstrations, showcasing the supposed resilience of its people in the face of NATO aggression. These events were carefully choreographed and heavily publicized to create an illusion of widespread support for the Serbian government.

In addition to domestic propaganda efforts, Serbia sought international sympathy by highlighting the humanitarian consequences of the air campaign. The government actively encouraged foreign journalists to visit areas affected by NATO bombings, emphasizing the suffering of civilian populations. By doing so, Serbia aimed to portray itself as the victim and NATO as the aggressor.

Serbia also engaged in a disinformation campaign, spreading false narratives to discredit NATO forces. The government claimed that NATO was deliberately targeting civilian infrastructure and cultural heritage sites, accusing the alliance of war crimes. These allegations were often unsubstantiated and aimed at tarnishing NATO's reputation on the world stage.

The effectiveness of Serbia's propaganda efforts varied. While some segments of the global audience were swayed by Serbia's narrative, others remained skeptical and sought alternative sources of information. Nevertheless, Serbia's propaganda campaign demonstrated the importance of media manipulation in shaping public opinion during conflicts.

Understanding the propaganda efforts by Serbia provides historians with valuable insights into the complexities of Operation Allied Force. By examining the methods employed by Serbia, historians can analyze the impact of media coverage on public perception and the role of misinformation in influencing international opinion. This subchapter sheds light on the multifaceted nature of modern warfare and the challenges faced by NATO in countering Serbia's propaganda machine.

Media Influence on Public Opinion and International Support

The subchapter titled "Media Influence on Public Opinion and International Support" delves into the significant role played by media in shaping public perception and garnering international support during Operation Allied Force, NATO's air campaign against Serbia. This section aims to provide historians with a comprehensive understanding of the media's impact on the conflict and its consequences.

Media coverage during Operation Allied Force was instrumental in shaping public opinion both domestically and internationally. Through various mediums, including television, newspapers, and online platforms, the media disseminated information, images, and narratives that influenced how the conflict was perceived by the general public. Historians will gain insight into the ways in which media coverage influenced public sentiment and the subsequent international support for NATO's intervention in Serbia.

Propaganda efforts by both NATO and Serbia added a complex dimension to the media's role in the conflict. As historians delve into this subchapter, they will explore the strategies employed by NATO and Serbia to shape public opinion in their favor. By analyzing the content and tone of media reports, historians can assess the effectiveness of propaganda campaigns and how they impacted international support for the opposing sides.

Moreover, this section will shed light on the ethical and legal justifications for NATO's intervention in Serbia, emphasizing the concept of Responsibility to Protect (R2P). Historians will examine how media coverage influenced public understanding of R2P and the responsibility to prevent mass atrocities. They will also explore debates surrounding the media's portrayal of civilian casualties and collateral damage resulting from the air campaign, critically assessing the unintended consequences and the media's role in exposing or downplaying these issues.

Furthermore, historians will analyze the media's impact on regional stability and the long-term consequences of Operation Allied Force on the Balkans region. They will investigate how media narratives and coverage influenced political, economic, and social developments in the aftermath of the conflict. By understanding the media's role in shaping post-conflict perceptions, historians can better evaluate the lasting impact of Operation Allied Force on the region.

Ultimately, this subchapter will provide historians with a nuanced understanding of the media's influence on public opinion and international support during Operation Allied Force. By exploring media coverage, propaganda efforts, and the ethical implications of media narratives, historians can gain valuable insights into the complexities of this conflict and its broader implications for international intervention and media's role in shaping public perception.

Chapter 8: Impact on Regional Stability: Assessing the Long-Term Effects of Operation Allied Force

Political Consequences and Power Shifts in the Balkans

The subchapter "Political Consequences and Power Shifts in the Balkans" delves into the far-reaching effects of Operation Allied Force on the region. This section aims to provide historians with a comprehensive analysis of the political aftermath and power dynamics that emerged as a result of NATO's air campaign against Serbia.

The Balkans, a historically turbulent region, experienced significant political shifts following the conclusion of Operation Allied Force. The air campaign, which aimed to halt the ethnic cleansing and human rights abuses perpetrated by the Serbian forces under Slobodan Milosevic, had unintended consequences that rippled throughout the region.

One of the key political consequences was the fall of Milosevic's regime in Serbia. The sustained air attacks, coupled with the diplomatic pressure exerted by NATO and its allies, weakened Milosevic's grip on power. This led to his eventual overthrow and subsequent trial for war crimes by the International Criminal Tribunal for the former Yugoslavia.

Furthermore, Operation Allied Force had a profound impact on the political landscape of the wider Balkans region. It provided an opportunity for ethnic Albanians in Kosovo to establish their own self-governing institutions, leading to the declaration of independence in 2008. This move had ripple effects on the neighboring countries of Macedonia, Montenegro, and Bosnia-Herzegovina, where ethnic tensions were heightened.

The air campaign also had implications for NATO's relationship with Russia. The intervention in Serbia, which Russia vehemently opposed, strained relations between the two powers and heightened geopolitical tensions in the region. This shift in power dynamics had long-lasting consequences for the stability of the Balkans and beyond.

Additionally, Operation Allied Force highlighted the limitations of military intervention and the challenges of achieving stability through force alone. The campaign demonstrated that political solutions and long-term diplomatic efforts were crucial in preventing further conflict and ensuring the region's stability.

In conclusion, the subchapter "Political Consequences and Power Shifts in the Balkans" offers historians a comprehensive analysis of the aftermath of Operation Allied Force. It highlights the fall of Milosevic's regime, the establishment of self-governance in Kosovo, the impact on regional stability, and the strained relations between NATO and Russia. This subchapter explores the complex and multifaceted political consequences that emerged from NATO's air campaign against Serbia, providing valuable insights into the long-term effects of military interventions in the region.

Economic Challenges and Reconstruction Efforts

During Operation Allied Force, NATO's air campaign against Serbia, the targeting of military infrastructure played a crucial role in achieving strategic objectives. This subchapter delves into the specific targets and objectives of NATO's air campaign, including the destruction of strategic bridges, communication centers, and military installations. By crippling Serbia's military capabilities, NATO aimed to weaken the regime's ability to carry out aggressive actions and force them to negotiate a resolution.

However, the air campaign also had unintended consequences, particularly in terms of civilian casualties and collateral damage. This section explores the ethical and moral challenges posed by these unintended outcomes, as well as the impact on civilian populations and infrastructure. It raises questions about the balance between military necessity and the protection of innocent lives, shedding light on the complexities of modern warfare.

Diplomatic efforts and negotiations were a critical component of Operation Allied Force. This chapter analyzes the challenges faced by NATO and its member countries in their diplomatic endeavors, including negotiations with Serbia and various international allies. It highlights the intricacies of diplomatic negotiations during a military campaign and underscores the importance of multilateral cooperation in addressing international crises.

The role of technology in the air campaign is another significant aspect explored in this subchapter. It examines the advanced military technology employed by NATO forces, such as surveillance systems, precision-guided munitions, and air superiority capabilities. Understanding the role of technology provides insights into the evolving nature of warfare and the increasing reliance on sophisticated weaponry.

Moreover, this section discusses the ethical and legal justifications for NATO's intervention in Serbia, with a particular focus on the concept of the Responsibility to Protect (R2P) and the responsibility to prevent mass atrocities. By exploring the humanitarian intervention aspect of the air campaign, it prompts a deeper understanding of the ethical considerations and legal frameworks that underpin such military actions.

The media played a significant role in shaping public perception of the air campaign. This subchapter investigates the media coverage and propaganda efforts employed by both NATO and Serbia. It explores how information was disseminated, manipulated, and used as a tool to influence public opinion, shedding light on the complexities of media warfare and its impact on public perception.

Furthermore, the long-term effects of Operation Allied Force on regional stability are assessed. This section analyzes the political, economic, and social consequences of the air campaign on the Balkans region. It provides valuable insights into the complexities of post-conflict reconstruction and the challenges faced in achieving lasting stability.

NATO's military strategy and tactics are extensively analyzed, covering the overarching military strategy employed during the air campaign. This includes the coordination of air assets, target selection, and operational effectiveness. By examining the military approach, historians can gain a comprehensive understanding of the planning and execution of the campaign.

Additionally, this chapter evaluates the lessons learned from Operation Allied Force and its impact on subsequent military doctrines and strategies. By reflecting on the campaign's successes and failures, it provides valuable insights into the evolution of air warfare and the development of new military strategies.

Lastly, the involvement of non-NATO countries in the air campaign against Serbia is explored. This section examines the participation of countries like Australia and New Zealand and their contributions to the overall mission. By highlighting the international collaboration, it underscores the significance of collective security efforts in addressing global challenges.

Social Repercussions and Ethnic Tensions

Operation Allied Force: The Untold Story of NATO's Air Campaign Against Serbia

Introduction:

As historians delve into the intricacies of Operation Allied Force, it becomes evident that the air campaign had far-reaching social repercussions and exacerbated ethnic tensions in the Balkan region. This subchapter aims to shed light on the multifaceted aspects of these repercussions, exploring the underlying causes, immediate effects, and long-term consequences. By examining the social and ethnic dimensions of the conflict, historians can gain a comprehensive understanding of the complexities surrounding NATO's intervention in Serbia.

Ethnic Tensions and Conflict Background:

To comprehend the social impact of Operation Allied Force, it is imperative to explore the underlying ethnic tensions that plagued the Balkans. Historians must delve into the historical context, dating back to the dissolution of Yugoslavia and the subsequent rise of nationalist sentiments, which ultimately led to the outbreak of armed conflict in the region. The deep-rooted ethnic divisions between Serbs, Croats, Bosniaks, and Kosovar Albanians laid the groundwork for the tensions that would be further exacerbated by NATO's intervention.

Repercussions on Civilian Populations:

While the primary objective of Operation Allied Force was to target military infrastructure and installations, civilian populations bore the brunt of the unintended consequences. Collateral damage, civilian casualties, and the destruction of vital infrastructure had a profound impact on the affected communities. Historians must analyze the humanitarian crisis that unfolded as a result of the air campaign, examining the displacement of thousands, the loss of lives, and the long-lasting trauma inflicted upon civilians.

Ethnic Polarization and Nationalistic Sentiments:

Operation Allied Force inadvertently fueled ethnic polarization and intensified nationalistic sentiments in the region. The air campaign, perceived by some as Western interference, prompted a surge in nationalist fervor among Serbs, exacerbating ethnic tensions and widening the divide between different communities. Historians must scrutinize the role played by propaganda and media coverage, as they contributed to the deepening of these divisions.

Long-Term Consequences on Regional Stability:

The social repercussions of Operation Allied Force reverberated long after the conclusion of the air campaign. Historians must examine the impact of the conflict on regional stability, including political, economic, and social consequences. The destabilization of the Balkans and the subsequent challenges faced by newly-formed states, such as Kosovo, highlight the far-reaching effects of the intervention.

Conclusion:

By delving into the social repercussions and ethnic tensions arising from Operation Allied Force, historians can paint a comprehensive picture of the air campaign's impact on the Balkans. The unintended consequences, ranging from civilian casualties to ethnic polarization, underscore the complexities of military interventions and urge the reevaluation of strategies to prevent further exacerbation of social divisions in future conflicts. Understanding these social dynamics is crucial for historians seeking to grasp the full extent of Operation Allied Force's legacy.

Chapter 9: NATO's Military Strategy and Tactics: Analyzing the Overarching Military Strategy Employed by NATO

Coordination of Air Assets

During Operation Allied Force, the coordination of air assets played a crucial role in NATO's air campaign against Serbia. The success of the operation depended on the effective integration and synchronization of various air assets from different NATO member countries. This subchapter aims to shed light on the intricacies of coordinating air assets and its impact on the overall military strategy employed by NATO.

One of the key challenges faced by NATO was the need to coordinate the efforts of multiple air forces operating in a joint environment. This required establishing common procedures, protocols, and communication systems to ensure seamless coordination and information sharing among the participating forces. The establishment of a centralized command and control structure, known as the Combined Air Operations Center (CAOC), served as the nerve center for planning, executing, and assessing air operations. The CAOC facilitated real-time coordination, intelligence sharing, and situational awareness among the participating air forces.

Effective coordination of air assets also involved the allocation and tasking of specific aircraft to fulfill different roles and missions. This included the deployment of fighter aircraft for air superiority, bombers for strategic strikes, and surveillance aircraft for intelligence gathering. The coordination of these assets required careful planning to ensure the optimal use of resources and the achievement of campaign objectives.

Furthermore, the coordination of air assets extended beyond the military sphere. It involved close collaboration with other components of the operation, such as ground forces and naval assets, to ensure a comprehensive and synchronized approach. This integration of air, land, and sea assets allowed for effective targeting of military infrastructure, communication centers, and other strategic objectives.

The coordination of air assets also leveraged advanced military technology to enhance operational effectiveness. This included the use of surveillance systems, precision-guided munitions, and air superiority capabilities. The integration of these technological advancements allowed NATO forces to conduct precise and targeted strikes while minimizing collateral damage and civilian casualties.

The coordination of air assets during Operation Allied Force demonstrated the importance of effective planning, communication, and integration in achieving military objectives. It highlighted the need for interoperability among different air forces and the utilization of advanced military technology. The lessons learned from this operation have since influenced subsequent military doctrines and strategies, shaping the evolution of air warfare.

As historians delve into the intricacies of Operation Allied Force, understanding the coordination of air assets will provide valuable insights into the operational effectiveness, challenges faced, and the impact of this NATO air campaign against Serbia.

Target Selection and Prioritization

One of the key aspects of Operation Allied Force, NATO's air campaign against Serbia, was the meticulous target selection and prioritization. This subchapter delves into the specific targets and objectives of the campaign, focusing on the strategic bridges, communication centers, and military installations that were targeted.

NATO's primary goal was to cripple Serbia's military infrastructure and disrupt its ability to wage war against Kosovo. By targeting key bridges, communication centers, and military installations, NATO aimed to sever the lines of communication and supply routes, weakening the Serbian forces and ultimately forcing them to capitulate.

However, the air campaign was not without unintended consequences. The impact on civilian populations and infrastructure, resulting in civilian casualties and collateral damage, raised questions about the ethical implications of the operation. This subchapter explores these unintended consequences and the challenges faced by NATO in minimizing civilian harm while achieving its military objectives.

Diplomatic efforts and negotiations played a crucial role in Operation Allied Force. NATO member countries engaged in diplomatic channels, both with Serbia and international allies, to seek a peaceful resolution to the conflict. This subchapter analyzes the diplomatic challenges faced by NATO and the negotiations that took place during the campaign.

The role of technology in the air campaign cannot be understated. NATO forces utilized advanced military technology, including surveillance systems, precision-guided munitions, and air superiority capabilities, to gain a tactical advantage over Serbian forces. This subchapter examines the role of technology in the success of the air campaign.

Furthermore, this subchapter delves into the ethical and legal justifications for NATO's intervention in Serbia, focusing on the concept of Responsibility to Protect (R2P). The responsibility to prevent mass atrocities and the humanitarian intervention aspect of the air campaign are discussed in detail.

Media coverage and propaganda also played a significant role in shaping public perception of the air campaign. This subchapter investigates the role of media in disseminating information and propaganda efforts by both NATO and Serbia.

The long-term effects of Operation Allied Force on the Balkans region are assessed, including political, economic, and social consequences. The impact on regional stability is analyzed to understand the lasting repercussions of the air campaign.

The overarching military strategy employed by NATO, including the coordination of air assets, target selection, and operational effectiveness, is thoroughly analyzed in this subchapter. Lessons learned from Operation Allied Force and their influence on subsequent military doctrines and strategies are evaluated.

Finally, the involvement of non-NATO countries, such as Australia and New Zealand, and their contributions to the overall mission are explored. The role of these non-NATO countries in the air campaign against Serbia is examined to provide a comprehensive understanding of the international coalition that participated in Operation Allied Force.

Operational Effectiveness and Lessons Learned

Operation Allied Force: The Untold Story of NATO's Air Campaign Against Serbia

Chapter 7: Operational Effectiveness and Lessons Learned

Introduction

In this subchapter, we delve into the operational effectiveness of NATO's air campaign against Serbia during Operation Allied Force. We will explore the specific targets and objectives of the campaign, the unintended consequences on civilian populations and infrastructure, the diplomatic challenges and negotiations faced by NATO, the role of technology in the air campaign, the ethical and legal justifications for intervention, media coverage and propaganda, the impact on regional stability, NATO's military strategy and tactics, lessons learned, and the role of non-NATO countries in the campaign.

Operational Objectives and Targeting Military Infrastructure

NATO's air campaign against Serbia focused on targeting strategic bridges, communication centers, and military installations. The objective was to degrade Serbia's military capabilities and disrupt their command and control systems. This subchapter delves into the specific targets selected and their impact on Serbia's military infrastructure.

Civilian Casualties and Collateral Damage

While NATO aimed to minimize civilian casualties and collateral damage, unintended consequences occurred during the air campaign. We explore the impact on civilian populations and infrastructure, analyzing the ethical implications and the challenges faced by NATO in mitigating these consequences.

Diplomatic Challenges and Negotiations

Throughout Operation Allied Force, NATO and its member countries faced diplomatic challenges and engaged in negotiations with Serbia and international allies. This section analyzes the diplomatic efforts made, the obstacles encountered, and the outcomes of these negotiations.

Role of Technology in the Air Campaign

Advanced military technology played a crucial role in the success of NATO's air campaign. We examine the surveillance systems, precision-guided munitions, and air superiority capabilities employed by NATO forces during the operation, highlighting their impact on the overall effectiveness of the campaign.

Humanitarian Intervention and the Responsibility to Protect (R2P)

This section discusses the ethical and legal justifications for NATO's intervention in Serbia. We focus on the concept of the Responsibility to Protect (R2P) and the responsibility to prevent mass atrocities, evaluating how these principles influenced NATO's decision to intervene.

Media Coverage and Propaganda

The media played a significant role in shaping public perception of the air campaign. We investigate the propaganda efforts employed by both NATO and Serbia, analyzing their impact on public opinion and the effectiveness of NATO's communication strategies.

Impact on Regional Stability

Assessing the long-term effects of Operation Allied Force on the Balkans region, we explore the political, economic, and social consequences. This section provides an in-depth analysis of the impact on regional stability and the challenges faced in the post-conflict reconstruction process.

NATO's Military Strategy and Tactics

Analyzing the overarching military strategy employed by NATO during the air campaign, we delve into the coordination of air assets, target selection, and operational effectiveness. This section provides insights into the decision-making processes and the tactical approaches used by NATO forces.

Lessons Learned and the Evolution of Air Warfare

Evaluating the lessons learned from Operation Allied Force, we assess their impact on subsequent military doctrines and strategies. This section explores how the air campaign influenced the evolution of air warfare and the adoption of new tactics and technologies.

Role of Non-NATO Countries

Lastly, we explore the involvement of non-NATO countries in the air campaign against Serbia. We highlight the contributions of countries like Australia and New Zealand, shedding light on their role in the overall mission and their impact on the campaign's effectiveness.

Conclusion

This subchapter provides a comprehensive analysis of the operational effectiveness and lessons learned from NATO's air campaign against Serbia during Operation Allied Force. By examining the specific targets, unintended consequences, diplomatic challenges, technological advancements, ethical justifications, media coverage, regional stability, military strategy, lessons learned, and the role of non-NATO countries, historians and enthusiasts of Operation Allied Force will gain a deeper understanding of this pivotal military operation and its lasting impact.

Chapter 10: Lessons Learned and the Evolution of Air Warfare: Evaluating the Impact on Military Doctrines and Strategies

Key Lessons Learned from Operation Allied Force

Operation Allied Force, NATO's air campaign against Serbia, yielded a plethora of valuable insights and lessons that continue to shape military doctrines and strategies. Historians and enthusiasts of military history will find this subchapter particularly enlightening as it delves into the key takeaways from this significant operation.

One of the most crucial lessons from Operation Allied Force was the importance of effectively targeting military infrastructure. NATO's air campaign specifically focused on strategic bridges, communication centers, and military installations. By targeting these critical assets, NATO successfully disrupted Serbia's military capabilities and conveyed a clear message of force.

However, the unintended consequences of the air campaign, such as civilian casualties and collateral damage, highlight the need for careful consideration of the impact on civilian populations and infrastructure. This chapter explores the complexities and ethical dilemmas associated with striking military targets while minimizing harm to non-combatants.

Diplomatic challenges and negotiations played a pivotal role in Operation Allied Force. The book examines the diplomatic efforts made by NATO and its member countries, including negotiations with Serbia and international allies. Understanding the diplomacy behind the operation provides insight into the intricacies of coalition warfare and the importance of international cooperation.

The role of technology in the air campaign cannot be understated. The chapter investigates the advanced military technology employed by NATO forces, such as surveillance systems, precision-guided munitions, and air superiority capabilities. This exploration sheds light on the ever-evolving nature of warfare and the critical role technology plays in achieving strategic objectives.

Another significant aspect of Operation Allied Force was the concept of humanitarian intervention and the Responsibility to Protect (R2P). The book delves into the ethical and legal justifications for NATO's intervention in Serbia, with a particular focus on the responsibility to prevent mass atrocities. This analysis provides a deeper understanding of the moral considerations involved in military interventions.

The role of media and propaganda in shaping public perception of the air campaign is also a crucial lesson from Operation Allied Force. Investigating the various propaganda efforts by both NATO and Serbia highlights the power of media in influencing public opinion during conflicts.

Furthermore, assessing the long-term effects of Operation Allied Force on regional stability, including political, economic, and social consequences, is essential in understanding the broader impact of military interventions. This examination provides valuable insights into the complexities of post-conflict reconstruction and stability.

The subchapter also evaluates NATO's military strategy and tactics, analyzing the coordination of air assets, target selection, and operational effectiveness. Understanding the overarching military approach employed by NATO during the air campaign allows for a comprehensive assessment of the mission's success and areas for improvement.

Finally, exploring the involvement of non-NATO countries, such as Australia and New Zealand, and their contributions to the overall mission sheds light on the global nature of the conflict and the importance of international cooperation in achieving strategic objectives.

In conclusion, this subchapter on the key lessons learned from Operation Allied Force provides historians and readers interested in military history with a comprehensive analysis of the operation's various aspects. From targeting military infrastructure to diplomatic challenges, technological advancements to media coverage, and regional stability to lessons for future air warfare, the subchapter offers valuable insights into this significant NATO campaign.

Changes in Air Warfare Tactics and Technology

In the subchapter titled "Changes in Air Warfare Tactics and Technology," we delve into the evolution of air warfare during Operation Allied Force, NATO's air campaign against Serbia. This chapter is aimed at historians and those interested in the intricacies of military operations.

During the conflict, NATO forces employed various new tactics and technologies that revolutionized air warfare. The use of precision-guided munitions allowed for more accurate targeting of military infrastructure, such as strategic bridges, communication centers, and military installations. This approach increased operational effectiveness while minimizing civilian casualties and collateral damage. We explore the specific targets and objectives of NATO's air campaign, shedding light on the strategic decision-making process behind each operation.

Moreover, we cannot ignore the unintended consequences of the air campaign. Civilian casualties and collateral damage were inevitable, and we analyze the impact of these unintended outcomes on civilian populations and infrastructure. This discussion delves into the ethical and legal implications of humanitarian intervention, focusing on the concept of the Responsibility to Protect (R2P) and the responsibility to prevent mass atrocities.

The subchapter also delves into the role of technology in the air campaign. Advanced surveillance systems provided NATO forces with real-time intelligence, while air superiority capabilities ensured their dominance in the skies. We examine the technological advancements that contributed to NATO's military advantage and their impact on the overall outcome of the campaign.

Furthermore, we explore the diplomatic challenges faced by NATO and its member countries during Operation Allied Force. Negotiations with Serbia and international allies played a crucial role in shaping the campaign's trajectory. By analyzing these diplomatic efforts, we gain insight into the complexities of international relations during times of conflict.

Additionally, we investigate the media's role in shaping public perception of the air campaign. Both NATO and Serbia engaged in propaganda efforts to control the narrative surrounding the conflict. We assess the impact of media coverage on public opinion and the dissemination of information.

Finally, we assess the long-term effects of Operation Allied Force on the Balkans region. This includes analyzing the political, economic, and social consequences of the air campaign and its impact on regional stability.

In conclusion, this subchapter delves into the changes in air warfare tactics and technology that emerged during Operation Allied Force. By evaluating the military strategy, role of technology, and diplomatic challenges, we provide a comprehensive analysis of NATO's air campaign against Serbia. Additionally, we draw lessons from this conflict and examine its influence on subsequent military doctrines and strategies. Finally, we explore the contributions of non-NATO countries, such as Australia and New Zealand, to the overall mission, highlighting the international cooperation involved in this historic operation.

Influence on Future Military Interventions and Operations

The air campaign against Serbia during Operation Allied Force had a significant impact on future military interventions and operations. This subchapter examines the lasting effects of the campaign and its implications for the conduct of warfare.

One of the key influences of Operation Allied Force was its targeting of military infrastructure. NATO's air campaign focused on specific targets such as strategic bridges, communication centers, and military installations. This approach demonstrated the effectiveness of precision-guided munitions and the importance of disrupting enemy command and control systems. Future military interventions would take note of these tactics and prioritize similar targets to cripple the enemy's capabilities.

However, the unintended consequences of the air campaign also had a lasting impact. Civilian casualties and collateral damage raised ethical concerns and sparked debates about the proportionality of military actions. The unintended harm caused to civilian populations and infrastructure highlighted the importance of minimizing civilian harm in future operations, leading to a greater emphasis on precision and accuracy.

Diplomatic challenges and negotiations played a crucial role in Operation Allied Force. The diplomatic efforts made by NATO and its member countries, including negotiations with Serbia and international allies, highlighted the need for diplomatic engagement alongside military action. This recognition of the importance of diplomacy in military interventions would shape future operations, emphasizing the need for a comprehensive approach.

The role of technology in the air campaign was another influential factor. The advanced military technology used by NATO forces, including surveillance systems, precision-guided munitions, and air superiority capabilities, showcased the importance of technological superiority in modern warfare. This would influence subsequent military doctrines and strategies, with a greater emphasis on incorporating advanced technology into military operations.

Operation Allied Force also raised important questions about humanitarian intervention and the Responsibility to Protect (R2P). The ethical and legal justifications for NATO's intervention in Serbia, focusing on the concept of R2P and the responsibility to prevent mass atrocities, would shape future interventions and the criteria for military action.

The media coverage and propaganda surrounding Operation Allied Force were also influential. The role of media in shaping public perception of the air campaign, including propaganda efforts by both NATO and Serbia, highlighted the importance of information warfare in modern conflicts. This would lead to a greater understanding of the power of media and the need for effective communication strategies in future military operations.

The long-term effects of Operation Allied Force on regional stability were also significant. The campaign's impact on the Balkans region, including political, economic, and social consequences, would shape future approaches to post-conflict reconstruction and stabilization efforts.

The overarching military strategy employed by NATO during the air campaign, including the coordination of air assets, target selection, and operational effectiveness, provided valuable lessons for future military interventions. These lessons would contribute to the evolution of air warfare and the development of new doctrines and strategies.

Lastly, the involvement of non-NATO countries in the air campaign against Serbia, such as Australia and New Zealand, highlighted the importance of international cooperation and coalition-building in military interventions. This would influence future operations, with a greater emphasis on multilateral cooperation and the pooling of resources.

In conclusion, Operation Allied Force had a profound influence on future military interventions and operations. The targeting of military infrastructure, the unintended consequences on civilian populations, diplomatic challenges, the role of technology, ethical considerations, media coverage, regional stability, military strategy, lessons learned, and the involvement of non-NATO countries all shaped the conduct of warfare in the years to come. Historians studying Operation Allied Force and its aftermath will gain valuable insights into the evolution of military doctrines, strategies, and the complexities of modern warfare.

Chapter 11: Role of Non-NATO Countries: Exploring the Involvement of Non-NATO Countries in the Air Campaign Against Serbia

Australia's Contribution to the Mission

Australia played a significant role in Operation Allied Force, NATO's air campaign against Serbia. Despite being a non-NATO country, Australia made valuable contributions to the overall mission, showcasing its commitment to international security and its willingness to support its allies in times of need.

One of Australia's primary contributions was its deployment of Royal Australian Air Force (RAAF) assets to the region. The RAAF deployed a number of fighter aircraft, including F/A-18 Hornets, to participate in combat operations. These highly advanced aircraft provided crucial air superiority capabilities to NATO forces, ensuring the safety and effectiveness of their missions.

In addition to its military contributions, Australia also played a key role in providing logistical support to the NATO campaign. Australian ships were deployed to the Adriatic Sea to assist with maritime operations, including the enforcement of an arms embargo against Serbia. This logistical support was vital in maintaining the flow of supplies and resources to NATO forces throughout the campaign.

Australia also made significant diplomatic efforts during Operation Allied Force. The Australian government worked closely with NATO and its member countries to coordinate their actions and ensure a unified approach to the conflict. Australian diplomats engaged in negotiations with Serbia and other international allies, advocating for a peaceful resolution and working towards a diplomatic solution.

Furthermore, Australia actively participated in the humanitarian intervention aspect of the mission. The concept of the Responsibility to Protect (R2P) was a key driver for Australia's involvement, as the country recognized the ethical and legal justifications for intervening in order to prevent mass atrocities. Australian forces played a crucial role in minimizing civilian casualties and collateral damage, demonstrating their commitment to upholding international humanitarian law.

Australia's involvement in Operation Allied Force had a lasting impact on the country's military doctrine and strategies. The lessons learned from the campaign influenced Australia's approach to future military operations, emphasizing the importance of advanced technology, coordination with international allies, and the need for a comprehensive diplomatic effort.

In conclusion, Australia's contribution to Operation Allied Force was significant and multifaceted. The deployment of RAAF assets, logistical support, diplomatic efforts, and commitment to the principles of R2P showcased Australia's dedication to international security and its willingness to play an active role in global conflicts. The involvement of non-NATO countries like Australia and New Zealand highlighted the importance of international cooperation and collective security in addressing complex regional challenges.

New Zealand's Involvement and Support

Operation Allied Force, NATO's air campaign against Serbia, was a complex and multifaceted military operation that involved the participation of various countries. One such country that played a significant role in this campaign was New Zealand. Despite not being a member of NATO, New Zealand demonstrated its commitment to international peace and security by actively supporting and contributing to the mission.

New Zealand's involvement in Operation Allied Force can be traced back to its longstanding tradition of supporting multilateral efforts to maintain peace and stability. As a staunch advocate of international law and the United Nations, New Zealand recognized the need to address the humanitarian crisis unfolding in the Balkans and prevent further atrocities. In this context, New Zealand deployed a contingent of highly skilled and professional military personnel to contribute to the NATO-led operation.

The New Zealand Defense Force (NZDF) made a valuable contribution to the air campaign by providing vital support in various areas. One key aspect of their involvement was the deployment of specialized personnel who operated advanced surveillance systems. These systems played a crucial role in gathering intelligence and identifying strategic targets for NATO forces. The NZDF's expertise in this area greatly enhanced the overall effectiveness of the air campaign.

Moreover, New Zealand also made significant contributions to the mission through its provision of air assets. The Royal New Zealand Air Force (RNZAF) deployed a squadron of fighter aircraft that conducted numerous sorties in support of NATO's objectives. These aircraft, equipped with precision-guided munitions, played a pivotal role in targeting key military installations, such as communication centers and strategic bridges.

New Zealand's involvement in Operation Allied Force was not limited to military contributions alone. The country also played an active role in diplomatic efforts to resolve the conflict. New Zealand engaged in negotiations with Serbia and other international allies, seeking to find a peaceful resolution to the crisis. This diplomatic engagement demonstrated New Zealand's commitment to pursuing a multifaceted approach to conflict resolution.

The participation of New Zealand in Operation Allied Force highlighted the importance of international cooperation and collective security. Despite not being a NATO member, New Zealand's contribution to the air campaign demonstrated its commitment to upholding the principles of peace, security, and the responsibility to protect. The involvement of non-NATO countries like New Zealand and Australia showcased the global nature of the operation and the broad support it received.

In conclusion, New Zealand's involvement and support in Operation Allied Force were significant contributions to NATO's air campaign against Serbia. Through their deployment of specialized personnel, provision of air assets, and active diplomatic engagement, New Zealand demonstrated its commitment to international peace and security. The country's participation highlighted the importance of international cooperation and collective security in addressing humanitarian crises and preventing mass atrocities. New Zealand's role in this campaign serves as a reminder of the global nature of conflicts and the need for collaboration among nations to maintain peace and stability.

Collaborative Efforts and Contributions to the Overall Mission

In the subchapter titled "Collaborative Efforts and Contributions to the Overall Mission," we delve into the significant role of collaboration and the collective contributions made by NATO and its member countries during Operation Allied Force: NATO's Air Campaign Against Serbia. This chapter aims to provide historians with a comprehensive understanding of the collaborative efforts that were crucial to the success of the mission.

Operation Allied Force was a prime example of the power of collaboration among nations. NATO's member countries, recognizing the need for a unified response to the crisis in the Balkans, pooled their resources and expertise to execute a comprehensive air campaign against Serbia. The contributions of each member country played a pivotal role in achieving the overall mission objectives.

One of the key aspects of collaboration was the sharing of intelligence and resources. Member countries shared vital information regarding Serbian military installations, infrastructure, and communication centers, allowing for precision targeting. The coordination of air assets, target selection, and operational effectiveness were all crucial elements of NATO's military strategy. Through collaborative efforts, NATO was able to maximize the impact of its air campaign.

Furthermore, the involvement of non-NATO countries, such as Australia and New Zealand, added a global dimension to the collaborative efforts. These countries, recognizing the importance of maintaining regional stability and upholding international norms, made significant contributions to the overall mission. Their participation showcased the broader international support for NATO's intervention in Serbia.

Collaboration extended beyond the military domain. Diplomatic efforts and negotiations were crucial in garnering international support and managing the complex dynamics of the conflict. NATO and its member countries engaged in diplomatic dialogue with Serbia and international allies to find a peaceful resolution. The success of these diplomatic endeavors was instrumental in achieving the mission's objectives.

This subchapter also explores the lessons learned from Operation Allied Force and its impact on subsequent military doctrines and strategies. The collaborative nature of the mission highlighted the importance of international cooperation in tackling complex security challenges. The evolution of air warfare, advancements in military technology, and the ethical and legal justifications for intervention were all areas profoundly influenced by this operation.

Ultimately, the collaborative efforts and contributions made by NATO and its member countries were critical in achieving the objectives of Operation Allied Force. This subchapter aims to shed light on the significance of collaboration in addressing complex crises and the enduring impact of these collective efforts. By understanding the collaborative nature of this air campaign, historians can gain valuable insights into the dynamics of international cooperation in the face of complex security challenges.

Note: This book outline is structured in a logical sequence that covers various aspects of the topic while catering to the needs of historians. However, the order and content of the chapters can be adjusted based on the author's preferences and research findings.

In this subchapter of "Operation Allied Force: The Untold Story of NATO's Air Campaign Against Serbia," we delve into the specific needs of historians and provide an overview of the book's structure. While the chapters are ordered in a logical sequence, it is important to note that the author has the flexibility to adjust the order and content based on their preferences and research findings.

The book aims to offer a comprehensive examination of NATO's air campaign against Serbia during Operation Allied Force. As historians, you are interested in understanding the historical context, the military strategies employed, and the long-term consequences of such a campaign. This book addresses these interests by exploring various niches related to Operation Allied Force.

The chapters cover a wide range of topics, including targeting military infrastructure, civilian casualties and collateral damage, diplomatic challenges and negotiations, the role of technology in the air campaign, humanitarian intervention and the Responsibility to Protect (R2P), media coverage and propaganda, impact on regional stability, NATO's military strategy and tactics, lessons learned and the evolution of air warfare, and the role of non-NATO countries.

Each chapter provides in-depth analysis and insights, backed by thorough research and historical evidence. The book examines the specific targets and objectives of NATO's air campaign, such as strategic bridges, communication centers, and military installations, shedding light on the decision-making process and the effectiveness of these actions.

It also explores the unintended consequences of the air campaign, including the impact on civilian populations and infrastructure, highlighting the ethical and legal dilemmas faced by NATO forces.

Diplomatic efforts made by NATO and its member countries are analyzed, including negotiations with Serbia and international allies, shedding light on the challenges faced during the campaign.

The role of advanced military technology, such as surveillance systems, precision-guided munitions, and air superiority capabilities, is examined, emphasizing the impact of technology on the success of the air campaign.

The book also delves into the concept of humanitarian intervention and the Responsibility to Protect (R2P), discussing the ethical and legal justifications for NATO's intervention in Serbia and the responsibility to prevent mass atrocities.

Media coverage and propaganda efforts by both NATO and Serbia are investigated, offering insights into how the narrative of the air campaign was shaped and perceived by the public.

The long-term effects of Operation Allied Force on the Balkans region are assessed, including political, economic, and social consequences, providing a comprehensive understanding of the campaign's impact.

NATO's military strategy and tactics are analyzed, including the coordination of air assets, target selection, and operational effectiveness, offering valuable insights into the overall military approach.

The book evaluates the lessons learned from Operation Allied Force and its impact on subsequent military doctrines and strategies, shedding light on the evolution of air warfare.

Lastly, the involvement of non-NATO countries in the air campaign against Serbia, such as Australia and New Zealand, and their contributions to the overall mission are explored, providing a broader perspective on the international collaboration during the campaign.

Overall, this book aims to provide historians with a comprehensive and well-researched account of Operation Allied Force, covering various aspects of the air campaign and its historical significance. The chapters can be adjusted based on the author's preferences and research findings, ensuring the utmost accuracy and relevance for the target audience.